# A Writer's Work

Written by Diana Noonan
Photographs by Diana Noonan and Keith Olsen

MW01148616

Diana writes books for children. It's her job and she loves it! We asked Diana some questions about her work.

*Do you write all day?*

No. I write stories in the morning. During the day I work in my garden, and at night I answer letters from publishers and schools and from the children who write to me.

*Where do you write?*

I have a tiny office away from my house. When I am working, I pull the curtain so that all I am thinking about is the story I am writing.

I like writing on cold, rainy days best. I turn the heater on to warm my feet!

## What do you use to write?

I use a computer with a word processing program. I'm not a very good speller, so the computer helps me check my work!

I have a printer for printing finished stories, but some publishers like work sent to them on a disk.

## *Where do you get your ideas?*

Most of the stories I write are about things that have really happened and people I really know. Sometimes I change the stories a little to make them funnier or more interesting.

I worry that I will forget all the things I want to write about, so I scribble ideas in notebooks. I have notebooks all over the house and in the car!

Sometimes when I am driving, I have to stop so that I can write down an idea.

*Do you ever run out of ideas?*

Not very often. If I do, I go for a walk. I live beside the sea, and the crashing of the waves and the calling of the sea birds usually help me think of a new story.

Once or twice, friends have "given" me a story. My friend Rachel was only eleven years old when she told me a story that is now a book. My neighbor Hugh told me the story of his cow and how she swam out to sea. I turned that into a book, too!

## Who does the illustrations in your books?

It's the publishers' job to find the best illustrator for the book. Often I never meet the people who produce the wonderful pictures.

Sometimes my husband, Keith, illustrates my work. Working on a book together is lots of fun.

## Do you choose the titles for your books?

Usually, but publishers sometimes want to change a title. I try not to like a title too much in case it is changed.

*Do you ever get tired of writing?*

Never! I enjoy creating characters and getting to know them. By the time I have finished a longer book, I feel as though I have made new friends and been to exciting places.

When I visit schools, I enjoy meeting other writers and reading their work, too.

*What tips do you have for writers?*

Read a lot. It helps your own writing.
Keep a notebook of all your ideas.
Try writing about people, places, and
events you know well.
Think and talk about an idea *before*
you write about it.

I saw Diana Noonan. We went to the hall to see Dianas books. I like her books. She likes me so much because I drew a picture for her